Caterpillar Capers

Louise Spilsbury

Crabtree Publishing Company

www.crabtreebooks.com

Author: Louise Spilsbury
Editors: Kathy Middleton
Crystal Sikkens
Project coordinator: Kathy Middleton
Production coordinator: Ken Wright
Prepress technicians: Ken Wright
Margaret Amy Salter

Picture Credits:
Dreamstime: Nikhil Gangavane: pages 3, 10; Cathy
Keifer: page 11; Photowitch: page 19; Xiaobin Qiu:
page 17; Mykola Velychko: page 18; Amy Walters:
page 21; Helen Worthington: page 14
Shutterstock: cover; Airn: page 13; Hagit Berkovich:
page 4, Alexander Chelmodeev: pages 1, 15; Cathy
Keifer: page 16; Varina and Jay Patel: page 20; Sue
Robinson: page 7; Antti Sompinmäki: page 8; Luna
Vandoorne: page 6; Maryunin Yury Vasilevich:
page 12; Vblinov: page 5; Bershadsky Yuri: page 9

Library and Archives Canada Cataloguing in Publication

Spilsbury, Louise
Caterpillar capers / Louise Spilsbury.

(Crabtree connections)
Includes index.
ISBN 978-0-7787-7854-7 (bound).--ISBN 978-0-7787-7876-9 (pbk.)

1. Butterflies--Life cycles--Juvenile literature. 2. Caterpillars--
Juvenile literature. I. Title. II. Series: Crabtree connections

QL544.2.S65 2011   j595.78'139   C2011-900601-4

Library of Congress Cataloging-in-Publication Data

Spilsbury, Louise.
Caterpillar capers / Louise Spilsbury.
p. cm. -- (Crabtree connections)
Includes index.
ISBN 978-0-7787-7876-9 (pbk. : alk. paper) -- ISBN 978-0-7787-7854-7
(reinforced library binding : alk. paper)
1. Butterflies--Life cycles--Juvenile literature. I. Title.
QL544.2.S654 2011
595.78'9--dc22

2011001337

Crabtree Publishing Company

www.crabtreebooks.com   1-800-387-7650
Copyright © 2012 **CRABTREE PUBLISHING COMPANY.**
Published in the United Kingdom in 2011 by A & C Black
Publishers Ltd. The right of the author of this work has
been asserted.

Printed in the U.S.A./072011/WO20110114

Published in Canada
Crabtree Publishing
616 Welland Ave.
St. Catharines, Ontario
L2M 5V6

Published in the United States
Crabtree Publishing
PMB 59051
350 Fifth Avenue, 59th Floor
New York, New York 10118

Contents

Starting Out 4

My Egg 6

I Hatched 8

Growing Up 10

In Hiding 12

On the Move 14

Time to Change 16

I am a Butterfly! 18

Flying and Feeding 20

Glossary 22

Further Reading 23

Index 24

Starting Out

I started life as a tiny **egg**.
Then I became a **caterpillar**
and grew bigger and bigger.

What happened next?

I didn't just get bigger—I changed
into something new! What do you think
I changed into? Find out in my story.

Some caterpillars
are very spiky.

tentacles

Can't see!

Caterpillars can't see well, so they use **tentacles** to feel their way around.

Guess what I will be?

My Egg

My egg was very small. It was so tiny it was only as big as the period at the end of this sentence.

Sticky eggs

My mother stuck my egg onto a leaf to stop it from rolling away and falling off. Then I began to grow safely inside the egg.

My egg looked a lot like these.

All different

Caterpillar eggs come in different sizes and colors. Most are **oval**, but some are round.

Stick around!

I Hatched

When it was time to **hatch**, I ate a big hole in the egg. Then I slowly crawled out of the hole.

Hungry caterpillar

I was very hungry, so I ate the rest of the egg. Then I started to eat the leaf. I ate and ate, and grew and grew. Soon I had eaten nearly all the leaf!

Chomp, chomp

jaw

Jaws!

Caterpillars have **jaws** that slide from side to side to mash up their leaves.

Caterpillars eat a lot of leaves.

Growing Up

I grew so much that I became
far too big and fat for my skin.
When the skin felt too tight,
I just wriggled out of it.

New skin

Underneath I had a new,
stretchier skin. My new
skin felt a little damp at
first, but it soon dried
out in the sun.

Hold tight!

Too tight

When caterpillars change skins, it is called **molting**. Caterpillars grow and molt at least four times.

new skin

old skin

Caterpillars grow very quickly.

In Hiding

When I was a caterpillar I had to hide. Animals, such as birds and spiders, try to catch caterpillars. Then they eat them up.

Being green

I was lucky—no birds ate me. I was the same color as the leaf I lived on, so when I kept still, the birds couldn't see me.

Happy camping

Some caterpillars make tents to hide in. They make silk to build the tents.

Unlucky!

Birds eat some caterpillars.

On the Move

When I was a caterpillar, I often moved around in the dark. Birds could not see me moving, so I could go wherever I wanted to.

Heave ho

I pulled myself along on my legs. First, I pulled the back legs up to the front legs, then I moved the front legs forward.

Caterpillars can walk upside down.

Hooked up

Some caterpillars have hooks on their legs that help them to hold onto things.

hook

Yikes!

Time to Change

After four weeks as a caterpillar,
I found a safe place to rest.
Next, I made a sticky pad. Then
I hung upside down from it.

Hard case

Then I molted for the last time.
My new skin became a hard case,
and I started to change inside it.

Hold tight!

Stay inside

I stayed inside my hard, green case and changed for about two weeks.

I grew a hard, green case.

I am a Butterfly!

When I came out of my hard, green case, I had changed into something beautiful—a butterfly!

Here I come...
First my head and legs popped out of the case, then I pulled my body out. It was very hard work. Then I stretched out my amazing, colorful wings.

Look at me!

Other kinds of caterpillars change into moths.

Super scales

Butterfly wings have lots of tiny, square **scales**.

Flying and Feeding

Now I fly from flower to flower looking for **nectar**. It is a juice flowers make, and I drink it.

More caterpillar capers

Soon it will be time for me to lay my own eggs. Then the caterpillars that hatch from the eggs will enjoy their own capers!

Sip Sip

Party insect

A butterfly's long tongue curls and uncurls like a party blower.

long
tongue

Butterflies drink with their tongues.

Glossary

caterpillar Creature with a long, wriggly body and a lot of legs. Caterpillars turn into butterflies and moths.

egg Round or oval case in which a young caterpillar grows. Eggs are laid by female butterflies.

hatch When a baby animal or insect breaks out of its egg

jaws Parts of the body that open and shut the mouth

molting When an animal sheds its old skin

nectar Sweet juice made by flowers

oval Long, circular shape

scales Tiny, hard parts that make up a creature's skin

silk Smooth, delicate material

tentacles Long, thin parts on an animal's head that the animal uses to feel its way around

Further Reading

Web Sites

This Web site helps you identify caterpillars in eastern forests of North America:

www.npwrc.usgs.gov/resource/insects/cateast/ families.htm

Find all the answers to your caterpillar, butterfly, and moth questions at The Children's Butterfly Site:

www.kidsbutterfly.org

Books

Face to Face with Caterpillars by Darlyne Murawski, National Geographic Children's Books (2009).

The Life Cycle of a Butterfly by Bobbie Kalman, Crabtree Publishing (2002).

Endangered Butterflies by Bobbie Kalman and Robin Johnson, Crabtree Publishing (2006).

Eyewitness: Butterfly and Moth by Paul Whalley, DK Children (2000).

Index

birds 12, 13, 14
butterflies 18–19, 20–21

case 16–17, 18

eggs 4, 6–7, 8, 20

hatch 8, 20
hooks 15

jaws 9

leaves 6, 8–9, 12
legs 14–15

molting 11, 16

nectar 20

oval 7

scales 19
silk 13
skin 10–11, 16

tentacles 5
tents 13
tongues 21

walking 14–15
wings 18, 19

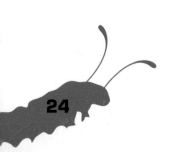